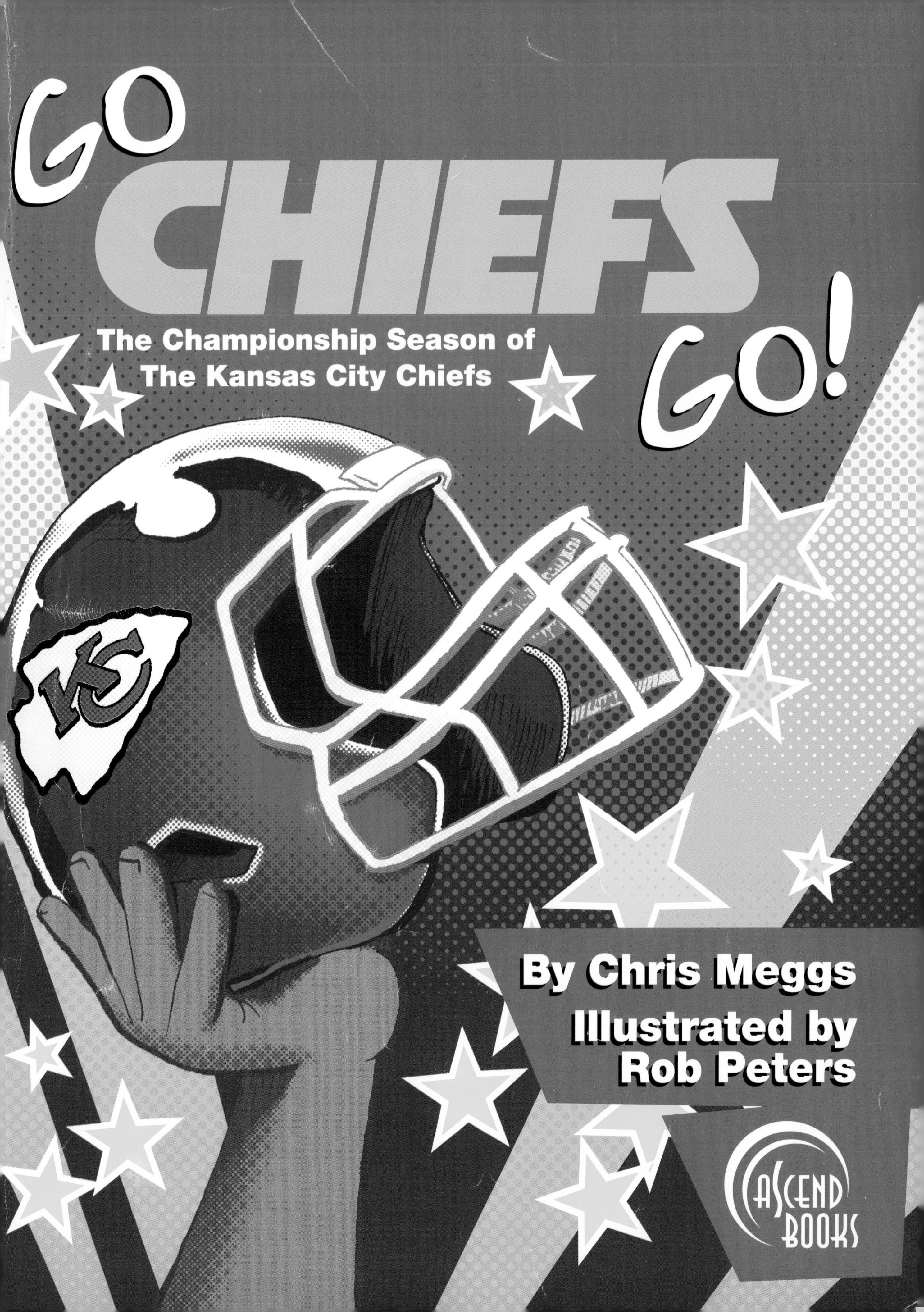
GO
CHIEFS
GO!
The Championship Season of
The Kansas City Chiefs
KC
By Chris Meggs
Illustrated by
Rob Peters
ASCEND
BOOKS

10 9 8 7 6 5 4 3 2

ISBN: print book 978-1-7344637-8-1
Library of Congress Control Number: 2020935475

Publisher: Bob Snodgrass
Editors: Julie Snodgrass and Teresa Bruns Sosinski
Publication Coordinator: Molly Gore
Sales and Marketing: Lenny Cohen
Dust Jacket, Book Design, and Illustrations: Rob Peters

Dedication

Thanks to my parents who raised me to
root for the best team in the NFL.
I hope this book forever captures the exciting victory
in Super Bowl LIV for the entire Chiefs Kingdom.
I also hope it helps inspire future Chiefs fans to
make Arrowhead Stadium even louder on game day.

—C.M.

Printed in Canada

www.ascendbooks.com

Listen everyone and you will hear
About the Kansas City **CHIEFS** and their Super Bowl year.
In the Chiefs Kingdom, expectations were high
And the Patriots loss last season was still **FRESH** in their minds.

It started with CAMP in the Saint Joseph heat
With a laser-like focus and no thoughts of defeat.
They learned every detail of all of the PLAYS
During preseason, they practiced perfection under
ANDY REID'S gaze.
KC

The day they dreamed of **FINALLY** arrived.
They were ready for the season opener with a gleam in their eye.
They started the season out on the road
Against the Jacksonville Jaguars ready to go.

Mahomes to Watkins sure was pretty
As Mitch Holthus shouted out
"TOUCHDOWN KAN-SAS CITY!"
Watkins scored two more times— what a beautiful sight.
And a 40 to 26 **WIN** started the season off right.

Up next were the Raiders in the Black Hole.
It was the last time we'd play there against our old foe.
MAHOMES was pure magic— four touchdowns he threw.
It was 28 to 10 for the Chiefs, win number ***TWO.***

Week number three was back in KC!
The Arrowhead DRUM beat as loud as could be!
For the home opener, the stadium was a big sea of red.
The LOUDEST FANS in the world cheered as
a bomber flew overhead.

The Baltimore Ravens came ready for a big game,
But the Kansas City Chiefs they just couldn't tame.
McCoy scored **TWO** touchdowns and the defense was true.
The Chiefs won 33 to 28 when it was **ALL THROUGH**.

The Detroit Lions were next on the list.
A game with two **UNDEFEATED TEAMS** not to be missed.
With time winding down, Darrel Williams ran in for the score.
The Chiefs celebrated **WIN** number four.

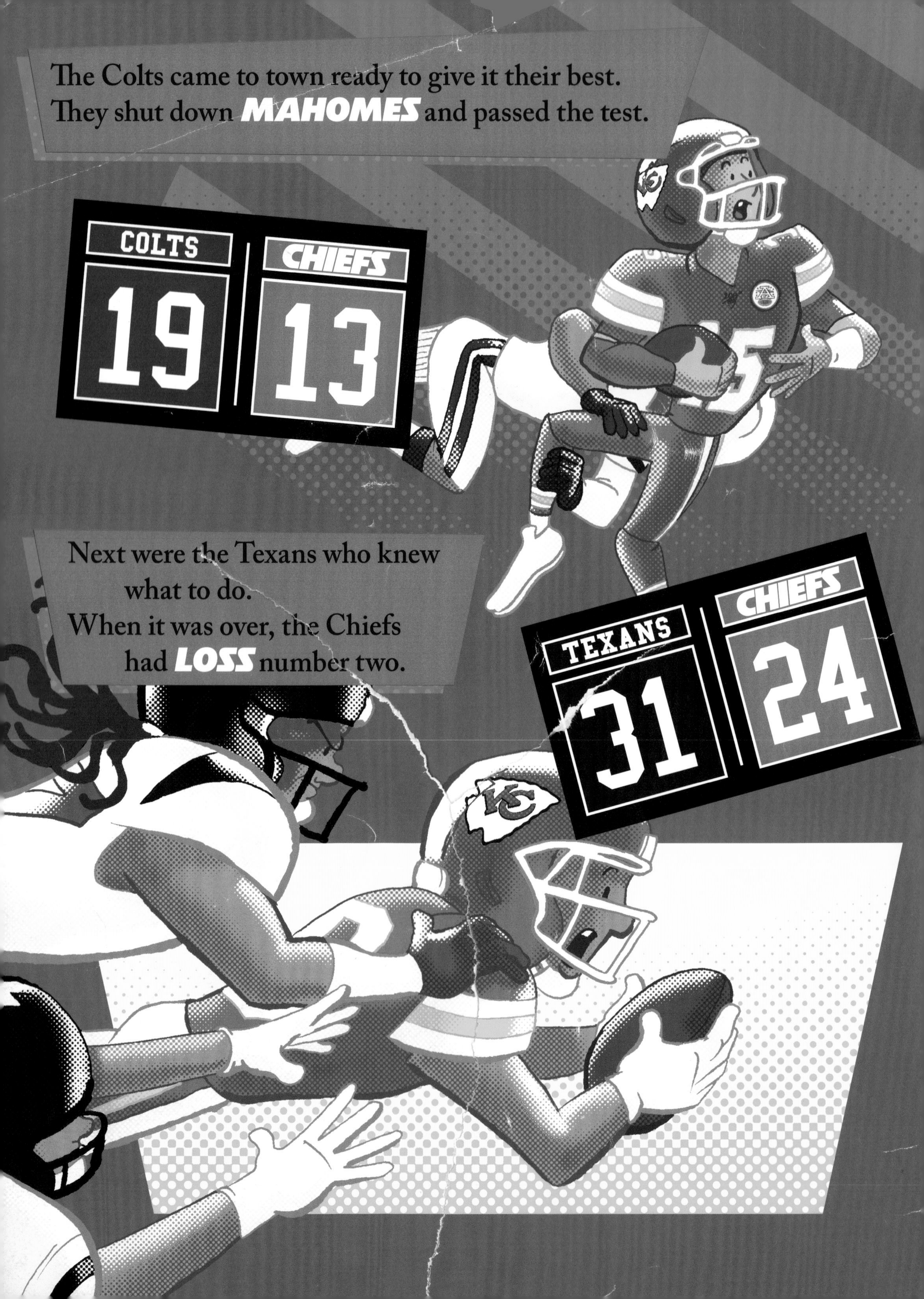
The Colts came to town ready to give it their best.
They shut down MAHOMES and passed the test.
COLTS
19
CHIEFS
13
Next were the Texans who knew what to do.
When it was over, the Chiefs had LOSS number two.
TEXANS
31
CHIEFS
24

The Chiefs went to Denver for a Thursday night game.
Mahomes got HURT— would the team be the same?
Ragland's fumble return and Moore's TD pass to Hill
Proved the Chiefs could find ways to WIN still.
CHIEFS
BRONCOS
30
6

Tony Gonzalez and Johnny Robinson were cheered at the next game.
Each was honored for joining the

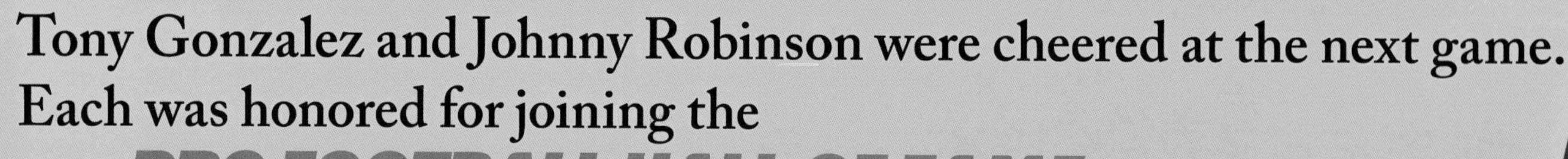

Aaron Rodgers and the Packers did the Chiefs in.
The Pack left Arrowhead Stadium celebrating a win.

The next game was against the men from up north.
The Chiefs and the Vikings went back and forth.
Butker kicked **FIELD GOALS** up, up and away
Including a last-second **KICK** that brought
victory that day!
7
7
VIKINGS
23
CHIEFS
26

Next, the Titans were ready to take on the Chiefs.
Mahomes was BACK! What a relief!
The Titans took the lead with a few SECONDS to go.
Then a blocked Chiefs field goal turned
fans' SPIRITS low.
CHIEFS
32
TITANS
35
7

The Chiefs weren't worried, they knew what to **DO.**
They picked off four passes that Philip Rivers threw.
In Mexico City, the Chargers they beat!
A goal-line interception sealed a **VICTORY** so sweet.

The Raiders came to Arrowhead in the bitter COLD.
The Chiefs offense was HOT and their defense was bold!
Mahomes threw a touchdown and ran for one more.
A POWERFUL WIN made the Kingdom's
hearts soar.
RAIDERS
9
CHIEFS
40

The Chiefs went to New England looking for **REVENGE.**
Last season's heartbreaking loss brought their
Super Bowl dreams to an **END.**
The defense was ready for Tom Brady's crew.
And they played with **HEART** the whole game through.

The Patriots' chances ended on a pass for the win.
The Chiefs stepped up to do the Pats in.
Breeland knocked it away and put on the clamps.
Making the Chiefs **AFC WEST DIVISION CHAMPS!**

Next up was Denver in the blowing KC **SNOW.**
The defense was stout. The Broncos had nowhere to go.
Hill scored two **TOUCHDOWNS.** Mahomes had a big game.
Kelce's fourth straight 1,000-yard season added to his **FAME.**

BRONCOS
CHIEFS
3
23

The Chiefs hit the **ROAD** to take on the Bears.
They worked really hard to make sure **VICTORY** was theirs.
Mahomes threw two TDs and ran for one amidst cheers.
Kelce became the **FIRST** tight end with 1,200-yards in back-to-back years.

In the season finale, the Chargers were beat
By two amazing plays that brought **FANS** to their feet.
Hardman had a 104-yard kickoff return
And Damien Williams raced 84 yards for a TD
with speed to **BURN.**

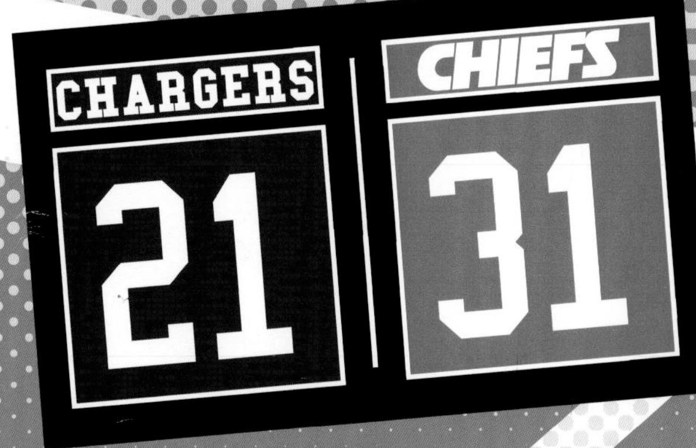

The Chiefs Kingdom ***CELEBRATED*** their season.
It was ***SPECIAL STUFF.***
However, winning the West was just not enough.

The playoffs were here and the Chiefs had a **HOME GAME.**
We wanted the **TROPHY** that bears our founder's name.

In the playoffs, the Texans jumped out to a 24-point lead.
Chiefs fans were wondering “how could this be?”
Mahomes worked his **MAGIC,** and boy did he **SHINE!**
Touchdown passes to **WILLIAMS AND KELCE**
sure did look fine.

The Chiefs continued to pile up the **POINTS**.
They were in a groove and would not disappoint.
51 TO 31 was the final that day.
The fans went crazy, the **SUPER BOWL**
was one win away!

The Tennessee Titans came to Arrowhead for another test.
The winner would be the **AFC'S BEST.**
The Chiefs rose to the challenge. It seemed like a dream.
The Chiefs had **WON!** They were now a
SUPER BOWL TEAM!

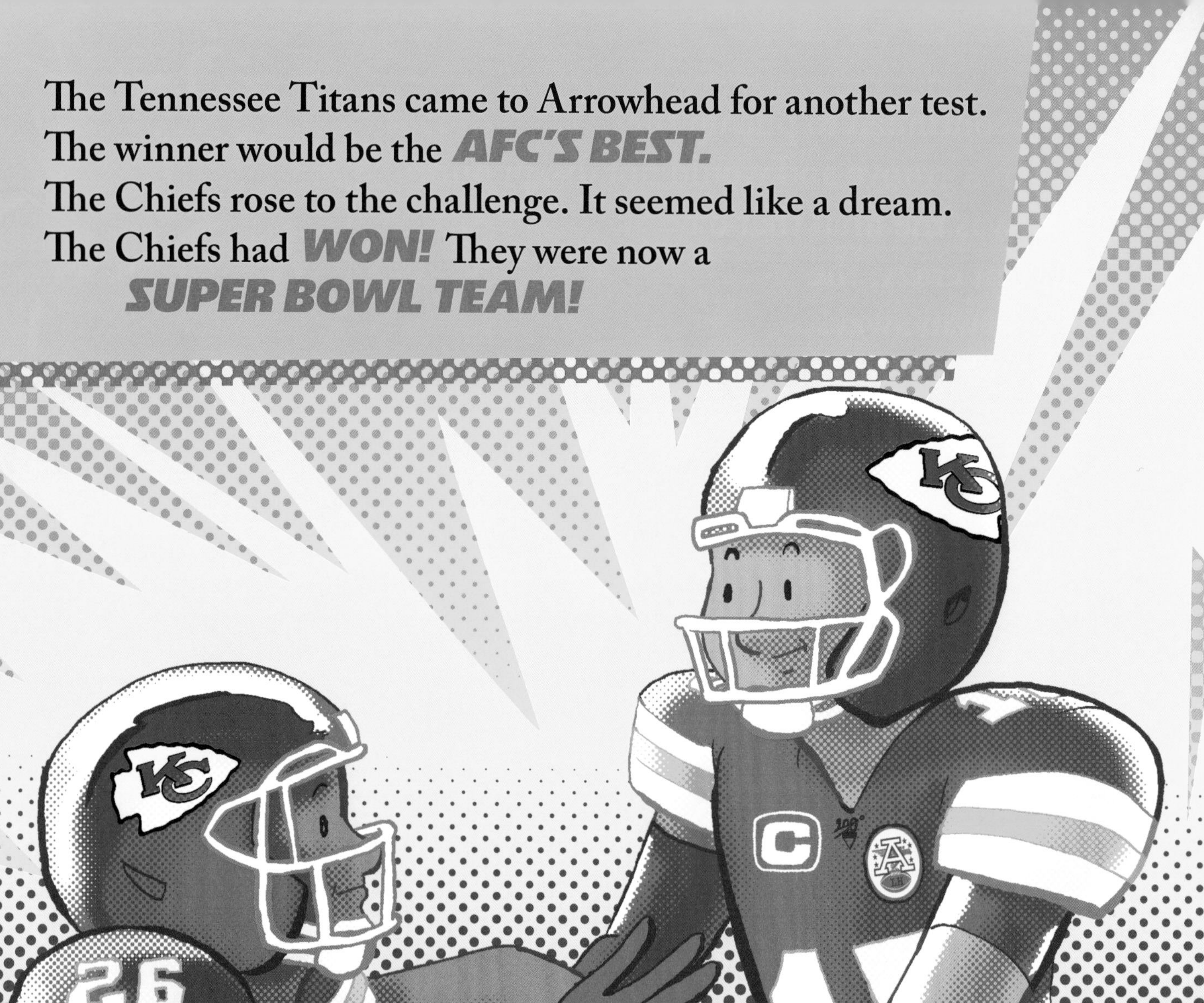

TITANS
24
CHIEFS
35

The **CONFETTI** was falling and **FIREWORKS**
exploded with light.
People were hugging and crying. What a **BEAUTIFUL SIGHT!**
The Chiefs had done it and were on the **AFC** throne.

And best of all, the Lamar Hunt Trophy
was ***FINALLY HOME!***

It had been **50 YEARS** since the Chiefs last Super Bowl game.
They beat the Vikings propelling Dawson, Taylor, and Bell to fame.
The **LONG WAIT** was over for a chance to **WIN**
the trophy once more,
But beating the 49ers in Miami would be a difficult chore.

While the team prepared, KC was bathed in **RED.**
Everyone knew there was **UNFINISHED** business ahead.
Chiefs flags waved in the sky so blue.
A Super Bowl **WIN** would be a dream come true!

Finally, in Miami, Super Bowl LIV was at hand.
Chiefs fans flooded the city and filled up the stands.
KC WOLF fired up the crowd with his antics and more.
When the Chiefs took the field, fans CHEERED with
a THUNDERING ROAR!
LH

The 49ers scored first with a field goal it's true,
But Chiefs fans **BELIEVED** Mahomes would come through.
He directed the team with **POWER AND SPEED**
And ran into the **END ZONE** to give KC the lead.

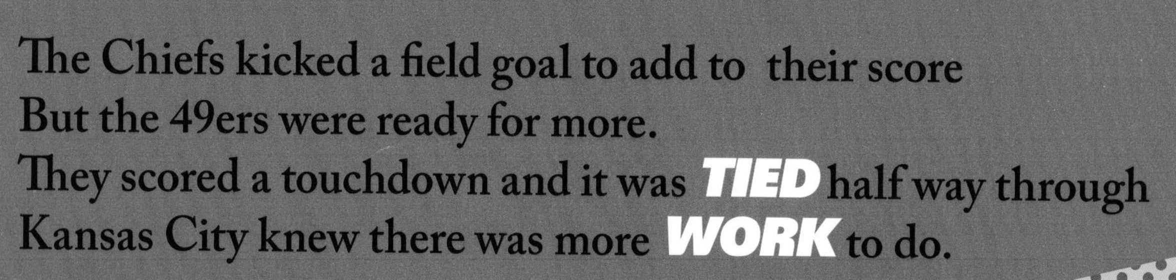

The Chiefs kicked a field goal to add to their score
But the 49ers were ready for more.
They scored a touchdown and it was **TIED** half way through
Kansas City knew there was more **WORK** to do.

The start of the **SECOND HALF** wasn't so nice.
The 49ers were able to score quickly, and twice.
They were ahead by ten and looked very strong.
The lead they built **WOULDN'T** last very long.

People were doubting if KC could win.
That's when MAHOMES' MAGIC really kicked in.
A TD pass to Kelce shifted the rally into gear.
Then another TD to DAMIEN WILLIAMS gave 49er fans fear.

The Chiefs had the lead and were back on **TOP.**
The defense was strong with stop after stop.
Williams scored again. It was **VICTORIOUS** indeed!
The team dumped Gatorade on Andy Reid.

The seconds ticked down and the **CONFETTI FLEW!**
Kansas City **CHEERED!** It was too good to be true!
After years of waiting, emotions
were hard to control.

The Kansas City CHIEFS
had just WON
THE SUPER
BOWL!

With the Lombardi **TROPHY** held high, the team returned to KC.
It was time to **CELEBRATE** with fans who were as happy as could be!
The city shut down for a **PARADE** that the Hunt family led.
The rally at Union Station was a huge sea of **RED.**

LIV
CHAMPIONS
LIV

It was a day that no one will ever forget.
And to this day, it's TALKED about yet.
Everyone joined ANDY REID in what he
had been saying for weeks,
"Come on now, let me HEAR you!
HOW 'BOUT THOSE
CHIEFS!!"